Potato Soup

Twyla Hansen

First Printing 500 copies July 2003
Second Printing April 2008

Cover Design, Typesetting, Book Design: Judith Brodnicki

The Backwaters Press

The Backwaters Press
3502 North 52ⁿᵈ Street
Omaha, Nebraska 68104-3506
gkosm62735@aol.com
(402) 451-4052
www.thebackwaterspress.homestead.com

ISBN 13: 9780-9726187-2-4

Acknowledgements

The Briar Cliff Review: "Veterans Day"; *The Cape Rock*: "This Early Evening"; *Crab Orchard Review*: "Prairie," "Scar," "White Lie"; *Credo*: "Endless Summer"; *Fine Lines*: "Monday, Snow," "The Morning After," "Morning Walk," "Saving Room"; *Flint Hills Review*: "Whole Summers"; *The Heartlands Today*: "On Medicine Bow Peak, Wyoming," "Unearthing"; *Karamu*: "Crane-Dance" (3rd Prize, poetry contest), "The Lesson," "Out Here"; *The MacGuffin*: "Classics," "Victoria's Secret"; *Midwest Quarterly*: "Just Before Dawn," "Late Winter, Survival"; *Nebraska Life*: "Underground"; *Nebraska Poets Calendar*: 1997– "Heron," 1998–"Just Before Dawn"; *The Nebraska Review*: "Winter Walk"; *Nebraska Territory*: "Building A House"; *New Delta Review*: "In Praise of the Temporal"; *Organization & Environment*: "At Rowe Sanctuary On the Platte"; *The Palo Alto Review*: "The Old Barn," "What I Did"; *The PlainSense of Things 2: Eight Poets from Lincoln, Nebraska*; (Sandhills Press 1997): "Just Before Dawn," "This Early Evening"; *Plains Song Review*: "Deer At Dusk," "We Are On Nine-Mile Prairie When"; *Platte Valley Review*: "Palimpsest"; *Poets Against the War* (Nation Books, 2003): "Veterans Day"; *Slant*: "Bones, Etc.," "Late Evening, Late Summer"; *Road Trip: Conversations with Writers* (The Backwaters Press, 2003): "Just Before Dawn," "My Husband Speaks of Wood," "The Snowball Sisters"; *Rural Mental Health*: "The Old Barn"; *Rural Voices* (Dirt Road Press 2002): "The Old Barn," "What I Did"; *SnowApple*: "Sunset on the Platte, Mid-March"; *South Dakota Review*: "Dust," "The Morning After," "What It Is"; *Talking River Review*: "My Husband Speaks of Wood"; *Times of Sorrow, Times of Grace* (The Backwaters Press 2002): "How My Doll Stopped Speaking to Me," "Monday, Snow," "Sumac Scattering Like Bones"; *Whetstone*: "Ducks Walking on Water"; *Whole Notes*: "Great Blue Heron Again."

"Crossing a Footbridge on Salt Creek, Early Morning in Mid-August," "Dovetails" and "Potato Soup" (all nominated for 2001 Pushcart Prize) reprinted from *Prairie Schooner*, by permission of the University of Nebraska Press, © 1999 University of Nebraska Press.

"We Are On Nine-Mile Prairie When" was film-illustrated by Nebraska ETV for *Next Exit* and was aired September 11, 2002.

Some of these poems were published in a limited-edition chapbook, *Sanctuary Near Salt Creek*, © 2001 Twyla Hansen by Lone Willow Press.

The author wishes to thank writing friends and others for listening, reading and helping shape many of these poems.

— to the Paulsens
& to Tom, Steve, Joei, Kathleen & Madelyne

Palimpsest

White Lie

Crossing a Footbridge

Coda

Palimpsest

POTATO SOUP

In the early years she helped her mother plant peels,
carry the dishpan out to the garden, digging holes.

What you eat is what you plant, her mother always said,
that edible tuber common as dirt, a near-daily staple.

One grandmother left potato country long ago for this one,
another immigrated for the promise of more potato land.

As she learned to cook, she began peeling alone at the sink,
sticking a spare slice on her tongue, smell of starch

lingering on her fingers. Mashed, fried, baked on Sundays
for hours, regular as pulsating winds over the plains.

Soon graduating to French fries in sizzling grease, to fermented
spirits of the potato. Beginning with a certain look in an eye,

relying on folklore, that time of the month safe if planted
at night under the expansive and unblinking moon. Grabbling

into the soil around roots to steal an eager potato or two.
She's fond of the skin color, the flesh, textures, exotic flavors.

Moving on to potato-salad years, quick-boiled varieties
from the hot tub. Decades here and gone; potato-love constant.

By now she's concluded it's best on gradual simmer, consolation
accompanying maturity. In the afternoon she sautés onion

and butter, stirs in flour and milk, chops celery, carrot, adds
chicken stock. She thinks of the hour when they'll be eating,

into twilight, of the long night ahead in front of the fire.
Should she throw in something extra, for tang, for play—

a measure of chardonnay? All her life, she thinks, it has come
down to this, bringing the bottle up slow to meet her lips.

THIS EARLY EVENING

This early evening he is on top of plywood
on top of what will be roof of the new addition,
crawling around, nailing down tar paper.

I cannot watch him lean toward the edge
with the round metal disks, hammer, nails.
I don't know why,

                    why at heights my legs
stiffen when I must descend, why I suddenly
feel heavy or clumsy or both.

Last year at the Anasazi ruins, tall ladders
taking us from one ancient level to the next.
He laughs at photos—*look, she's got a death grip
on that rung.*

Now's the time for deftness and buoyancy,
sweetness and light. The gravity of air,
not earth, balancing on the tip of a feather.
Think bird and wing, the parting of airwaves.

This early evening from a ladder on the edge
of the new roof, my knees weak, watching him,
and overhead, gulls circling,

                    circling and
turning, disappearing over the treetops,
the sun hitting their undersides as if cotton
hankies in the sky, floating,

                    soaring,
in early fall a gathering of robust gulls
going south, their webbed feet dangling freely
in the wind, along for the ride.

EARLY SEPTEMBER

Heated earth meets cooler morning air: fog.
I move through it into the roundness of things —
soybeans turning, cricket sounds, trees with their
trailing leaves. The heron returned to the creekbed.

Things, the biologist says, are becoming something
else — fry becoming a meal, chlorophyll cutting back,
insects anxious to mate. So when it happens
I'm not surprised: birds — blackbirds — in the hayfield,

a dark cloud rising and shifting, a restless black screen
against the fog, in silence moving this way and that.
At once I see father in his bee veil, at the center
of a swarm, calm, brushing the small bodies into a box.
And I, too, standing perfectly still, becoming small.

                          ***

No telling how long the hummingbirds will stay now.
Helicopter wings, hovering before the perch, before
the needle-beak dips into nectar. Late summer,
now the liquid feeder level goes lower each day.
Yet all I see are occasional wings, the nervous

comic flight. Things, the biologist reminds us,
are becoming something else. Before my eyes
transformation of sugar into energy — tree, shrub, vine,
sunlight and oxygen — this feeder hanging from a maple
imitating the deep throat of a flower.

Last night on top of Holmes Lake dam, at precisely 7:53,
the sun went down in flames. Muggy air, yet every so often
a breeze, giving it all away: this won't last. As it cannot,
the orange ball reflected in the young child's eyes,
her smile the one hope I hold out for.

THE SNOWBALL SISTERS

Behind me, behind the sofa
two little sisters stand styling my hair —
combs, bands and barrettes —
their tools put to serious use,
their voices from somewhere far in the back
of their blameless throats.

Reading the news, I try to picture it:
Earth, once a gigantic snowball.
There's now evidence our planet turned
so cold, oceans froze from pole to equator.
Half a billion years ago, for some ten million years.
Thawing then in a sudden greenhouse effect.

Their breaths, uttering tiny dictums, are cool
and sweet. Today the sun bears down,
a scorching sphere. Concrete a willing
and absorbing heat sink. Have we decided finally
more is better? The ozone shrinks.
I obey their every command.

Volcanoes, however, keep belching
carbon, the runaway glaciation cannot last.
I read faster. *Then, all hell breaks loose,*
the scientist says. *The meltdown is rapid.*
Evolution, we are told, speeded up, defining
everything: complex species.

In a few short months it will be winter,
the onward march. Glaciers wait patiently
on mountain slopes. Days shorten.
We will be cozy around the fire, or throwing
snowballs. Youth, as it was meant to be,
perfectly wasted on the young.

Worms and snails, meanwhile, burrowing
into the ocean floor, stirring up gases.
The younger one swipes at my bangs
with a brush. I am frozen in place. The older one
pauses, swatch of my hair in her hand, whispers
This will only hurt a little.

LATE EVENING, LATE SUMMER

Earlier, Canadian wind singing autumn
through feathertips, geese skimming
the gilt-edge crowns of hackberry.

This particular evening I am propped
on the bed with three plump pillows,
pen, pad, fatcat, the periodical
I browse holding its familiar names,
self-indulgence frequenting its pages.

On television the story of Wounded Knee
unfolding as deliberate and sad as rain,
historians theorizing both sides.

Tonight I grow weary of fairness,
of human failure. Sitting Bull's people
outnumbered, others joining them,
the false promises of a new religion,
a new life on the vanishing open plains.

In my bones I am weary of predictability,
of media poised and desperate for a story.
Do I hear the doorbell ringing?

The people of Big Foot in ghost shirts
before all those cavalrymen, dancing.
Outdoors, the unsettled sky, cottonwood
leaves dropping yellow and brittle,
warty-corked bark on hackberry darkening.

I want the army rifles to misfire,
the holy shirts on Sioux to shield them,
women and children to escape into ravines.

Instead, infamous photos of faces
and blood and bones over the snow
falling overnight at Wounded Knee.
The great-grandson of Big Foot
shaking his long, dark hair.

Historians defining massacre. Outdoors,
weather clouds on a long south journey,
threat of an unusually early frost.

PRAIRIE

There are those who think the prairie unimportant,
But this place, where soil and deep-rooted grasses meet,
Carries on —
Where hawks loop low into wind
Without wingbeat,
Where owls hide in cottonwoods,
Where dickcissels, in a swaying landscape,
Cling to seedheads,
Where the sun, to dictate each day,
Rises due east.

***

Now this remnant, now that, patches here and again
Across the Plains where great animals
Roamed, bones and blood of ancestors
Purloined for study, an entire region steeped in history,
Tribes and traditions and burial sites,
Hunting grounds and gathering places,
A civilized nation filled with story and survival
Dismissed as prehistoric,
Pre-European, pre-settlement, pre-plow,
Pre-grazing, pre-fences, pre-rifle.

***

A stiff breeze further bends the blanched grassblades,
Hairy sumac seeds, brownheaded lespedeza.
Underfoot — matted thatch. Beyond —
Switchgrass. And overhead — big bluestem.
The caws of blackbirds tossed into untamed air.
I cannot walk easily over this thick muslin.
I am hungry to remain, to get away.
Thirsty, yet these roots hoard all moisture.
Poor, in spite of verdant topsoil. I lie at ground level,
Carrying on, my face not at odds with, just now,
The rising sun.

SUNSET ON THE PLATTE, MID-MARCH

1.

Around the tree-thickened, dark-hued sandbars
the river ripples, swift-moving, near-silent, under me,
over rounded rocks past the willow-shore and stubblefields.

Sound builds beyond the wetland trees. A clamor.
Teals, geese, even a bald eagle in flight
at waning light, restless, searching.

At last, waves of wide wings from all directions,
dark against the dusk, cranes thick overhead
in formation to their roost, their night-watch.

2.

Under the first star we stand frail, frigid,
wind in the face reminding us just how weak.
Cloudless air, snow-melt water-chill,
nothing to block winter's last breath,
out here, middle of the unforgiving plains.

In a just-thawed channel, sandhill cranes
land with gusto, descending in droves
as they have always, by instinct returning
from feeding grounds to roost on the river,
fattening-up for the long journey.

3.

In the beginning, there were words — heaven
and earth — and all, they say, was good. But soon
it became even sweeter: soil, water, air, fire.

And it came to pass the smell of success
was not enough, became a gulp, a purple greed.
That what we took for granted would surely shrink.

The river is no longer untamed, no longer braided,
no longer flooding, no longer scouring, no longer

spreading out, no longer harmless. Even so, they come.

4.

Swirling, their numbers and voices swell, power-flyers
awkward on land, strength in numbers, en masse
in water. In this hour, in this neck-hair-raising eye-blink,
the flesh feels what the ear tells it: wing-swoosh,
gurgle-throat, echo-call, ancient tongue.

HERON

Above the dike, early sun divides
   the opposite bank into light and dark,
     sky reflected on slow-moving water.

Below, a great blue heron rises motionless
   on stilt-legs in the shallows,
     her bill as if a dagger poised.

There are theories, yet no one for certain knows
   how the first birds began flight—gliding from a tree
     or flapping off the ground—to escape or to eat.

All winter, walking to this creek,
   I have seen her standing in the unfrozen stream,
     gleaning.

A drift of snow lies protected on the steep,
   shadowy bank. Imagine millions of years ago:
     Archaeopteryx—Jurassic bird with clawed fingers,

teeth and bony tail like a dinosaur;
   no evidence of snow or ice anywhere,
     plant—animal—earth in a state of grace.

Later, she will fold her long neck, take flight without me,
   glide on ancient wings a few yards further,
     reaping this short cold day.

UNEARTHING

Chicago police say dying woman in Nebraska
confessed to her daughter's long-ago death;
friends, even family, didn't know. —news item

Here is the man digging his flowerbed,
discovering what the decades had concealed:
a skull — child's, her underdeveloped form
deprived of food, then oxygen —

on a December day, his ordinary arms
and shovel next to the apartment building,
intent perhaps on making the world brighter
or simply removing debris, when he heard

the thud, impact of metal on bone, his hands
going into grave, the soil's black secret.
Mild winter, air off the unfrozen lake, his pale skin,
his face and ungloved hands at this unlikely task.

Spading our own gardens how freely we breathe,
our hands grasping innocent tools. Even scientists
have not yet fully unraveled earth's mysteries,
the deep and complex workings of dirt,

or why the heart, in denial, holds its darkness,
its chambers divided, yet pulsing. Years ago
in my hometown I knew of a teenager abducted,
her wounded body abandoned in a field of alfalfa,

that next spring Sundquist on his International, then
the revelation from his high seat, the low sickle bar
intent on recovery. Brisk air through his open mouth,
over bones sinking into loam.

                    Some things
even years cannot erode. And somewhere a dying man
may open his mouth, the words of his confession
set loose, like a soul's, on some uncharted path.

MILK

When the waiter turns to me and I say *milk*
he mistakes it for *merlot*,
my companion having just ordered cabernet,
our dinner options delineated,

lights dimmed, the beautiful all about,
a sense that the authentic world is preoccupied,
and somehow I feel as if I have traveled here
from another country, a place time can't remember,

that patch of nameless property
where bovines outnumber domesticators,
so I repeat the word slowly, deliberately, lone
syllable that hints of a pace unhurried,

sun and rain and soil to pasture and ruminant,
green cud stirring gradually from one stomach
to the next, to the next, and then,
to the next.

BEFORE THE POEMS

Before the poems, there were the rocks
she collected and kept in a drawer.
These were the rocks of her youth,
hard-found in a land of deep loam,
exotic gifts, walking roads alone,
never straying too far, picking them up
like words to marvel at. Their surfaces
smooth or jagged, colors plain or curious,
fitting her palm. They were there, the rocks,
when she needed them, when the cattle
were prodded into trucks, carried away,
when the rendering truck came for
the caked and bloodied calf in the milk barn.
Rocks kept their silences, warmed or cooled
her hands, not once talking back or taunting.
All night a moaning from the windbreak,
the spruce trees that lifted their blue skirts
and took her under them unseen.
The world whizzed by, spraying gravel.
She'd run down the lane hoping a new rock
would reveal itself. There in the undulating hills,
among the ghosts of her grandparents,
in the middle of plowed fields that yielded
everything, the cribs filling with harvest.
Alone in the trees, rocks in her hands,
rubbing until it hurt, the time of year
when the wind sweeps relentless,
when branches move dark and bare.
Dig a hole and breathe dry earth.
She carried them — igneous, metamorphic,
sedimentary — silent and unblinking, storing
desire before she had a name for it.
All roads there ended in a cornfield.
All parents survived the Depression
and the War. Kids scoured creeks for anything
alive, crows, raccoons and cans all
potential targets. Did she believe
the rocks might save her, clamping her ears
when the bulldozer came? Examining roots,
then — odd tentacles exposed to sunlight —

trees sacrificed for a sight line, the county
intersection. Clapboard house sitting naked
to the world, then, headlights an odd movie
across her bedroom wall. Before her fear had
a name, before her body went hip and breast,
before she was aware of loss and lasting change.
The rocks secure in the top musty drawer
of a dresser that no one now remembers
what happened to. Rocks she will wonder
about years later, after the poems,
after the words strung themselves together
into lines, stretching from post to post and back,
on wash-day lines sagging under the weight
of their own wrung-out dampness, words
flapping in the wind through the decades,
after the whine of tires on city pavements,
the early songs of cardinals waking her,
a full-fledged cold-front moving in
for the duration.

JUST BEFORE DAWN

Just before dawn the great blue heron
glides its bony frame into the dusty light,
flapping slow above the russet field,
giant harvester inching through the rows,

its operator my father, perhaps,
pulling an ancient combine
behind an even older John Deere,
thin brown arms propped over its wheel,
his lungs wheezing, wiping his nose
with a rolled-up sleeve.

I can see his seedcap and work denims,
this scene replayed slowly ten thousand times,
following him after dark into the kitchen,
milking and feeding and fixing complete,

at the sink stripped to his boxers and undershirt,
washing with Lava the day's grit off
his leathery face and arms,
aroma of supper and sweat and soap,
his old-fashioned wire-rims and old country
references, hold-over from the last century,

not embarrassing me now—
flying above it all,
settling down onto shallow water,
body erect, senses alert, all alone.

THE FARM AGAIN

The farm again. Burt County.
My brothers on a pile of gravel playing king

of the mountain. Summer — cow dung, cottonwood
fluff. Morning carries effluvium of sweetclover.

I'm overhead watching, in the maple, through branches.
Youngest child, only girl, I crave attention,

yet at six know enough not to fiddle with harm.
If I try to stop them, they'll turn on me, fight

dirtier. I swallow back their names, those syllables
in my throat through the years lodged deep.

I cannot speak of fear, my unarticulated love.
A faceless hurt slugs its weight around, bruising.

Then as now. My older brothers climbing,
pushing, sliding — all fists and teeth — a bloom

of blood spattering on dungarees. Songbirds
keep their distance; I barely breathe. Shards of sand

fling to far corners. Things fall apart, the center cannot
hold, the mountain sinks. My hand reaches out,

pulls back. Our rural kingdom collapsing in a pile
of years. Then or now, will I never win?

LATE WINTER: SURVIVAL

First, attempt to describe the blackbirds, the plentiful
anonymous mass in the top of the cottonwood.

Begin with "black," "copious" and "red-winged," knowing
that anything specific will point only to more uncertainty.

They will perch there, noisy and prim, defying also
narration. Your mouth will be slack, your neck craned.

In the *Populus*, meaning prevalent, meaning of little
ornamental value, the tree that grew like a weed.

Forget the Canadian breeze, the chill that knuckles
your resolve, the snow deeper than recent memory.

It will bring to mind those monster drifts of old days,
how you and your brother climbed into the heights

of the shelterbelt, slid later into muck, the farmstead
and roads and countryside a sea of endless mud,

until summer, when the wind exhaled, the soil cracked
and you ached for rain. Oh, my child, how you dreamed!

And now this cackling confusion of starlings overhead,
the sun at a sharper angle, rousing the earth.

Not the songbirds you smile at, but a migrating pack
that grows darker with each passing day. Right now

the earth is tilted just so and the sunlight is brilliant
and everything, every last thing seems possible.

SCAR

       the one on mother's chest, noun
that taught me *scar*, raised stripe where a breast
had been, verb that meant something to fear,
that meant finding a lump in your breast, waking
after surgery with parts missing,
adjective that whispered shame and embarrassment,
my mother standing before me in that upstairs bedroom
pointing, saying *scar*, and I, maybe eight,
not understanding

       bedroom where I snooped
in dresser drawers, my father's rolled-up Sunday socks,
the woven-silk folded white scarf I never saw him wear,
the small wicker basket with the over-sized coins,
silver dollars big as my fist, the worn paper currency
that might as well have been foreign, all foreign to me,
his Masonic tie clasp and matching cuff links, the society's
secrets safe, then, buried with him wearing his one good suit
and the leather white apron

       place where I learned parents kept secrets
from their children, the walk-in closet reeking of mothballs,
the navy-blue dress mother wore in their marriage photo,
some days when father was in the fields, mother
downstairs or in the garden or brooderhouse,
I'd steal into that closet to slip the slimness over my head,
zip the bodice, prance in front of a mirror, at their vanity
dab on a little Evening in Paris, slender bottle blue
exotic and unknown

       careful not to apply too much
so she wouldn't wonder, and if she asked I'd say just playing
or some other fib, bedroom filled with the bare essentials
they'd owned since their wedding or before,
the Depression, my father the bachelor farmer caring
for his mother, my mother the impoverished teenager,
the difference in their ages melting away,
first one son, then another, and another, at last the girl
they'd wished for

          child to care for them in their old age,
my father teased, maybe, his blue eyes twinkling,
mother serious, her life not easy, now showing this scar,
this nightmare, to her only daughter, not explaining, leaving me
to wonder much later, recalling that scar, phoning her to learn,
once and for all, was it malignant — the lump? Benign.
But her breast was gone. And so I learned many things
to be uncontrolled — lives in poverty, bodies in the hands
of practitioners, secrets that small hands attempt to pry apart

WINTER WALK

The artist selects pink,
hot pink, orange; thick blue-gray
beyond the horizon, brighter tones
poking through the trees.

By now I have come to love them,
these walks in early morning alone,
the drone of traffic along Superior,
so safe here I can hike in the dark.

Sun not yet up, high-lighting cumulo-
nimbus cloud-pouches—mammata
like an inverted cushion, an egg-crate
foam—and at once I think of father,
that pad beneath him toward the end,
that last day when he couldn't speak.

I believe he would have liked it this way,
floating above us, his body weightless,
we would have known what we couldn't
that day, perhaps, by his unstrained face
it was okay to let him go.

Looking down—even the white leather
of my runners tinged pink, each step
traced pink, oncoming vehicles reflecting
pink, pink on billboards, on lightposts.

I listen to my breasts, slightly swollen
inside my sweatshirt, jiggling, a throb
in my lower abdomen—this body
capable of producing another child.
I can't imagine. Yet it goes on believing.

Wondering if mother truly wanted another—
last child of four—did she cry to get the news
early in '49? Father—himself a late child,
telling me what he most wanted after three sons
was a girl.

Late child of a late child. Who rebelled

and brought him disappointment, shame.
He lay there on foam, hardware hooked,
signals flashing, chest heaving.

Yet this morning for moments he floats,
looking down with his familiar grin.
The earth rotates. The sun muscles itself
awake. The artist chooses day-glo orange,

clouds yielding to blue-gray.
I'm roughly back at the house.
Another day is about to begin.

WHAT IT IS

It is not the headlight, breaking, not the sound
of glass on pavement, and not the pavement.
It is not the dawn, nor the whine of traffic, four
lanes of it, or the creek running through the fields.
It is not the road that leads her here, the creek
and fields of her childhood, it is not her childhood.
It is not the one dead face down in shallow water
from who knows what, but the one last week,
its bloodied and unrecognizable parts. What it is
is the worn story — man and nature — the odds.
It is the early morning, the sharp air, a walker lost
in reverie, a car not stopping. On the inside lane a doe
hitting concrete, that whump — like a brother and sister
fighting in the upstairs bedroom, pillows and feathers
flying — into something soft, fur scattering, it is the one
light punched out, the other intact and moving swiftly on.

BONES, ETC.

There is nothing in nature that can't be taken
as a sign of both mortality and invigoration.
— Gretel Ehrlich

Decades ago, they were there—
Asclepias, Liatris, Solidago—where each fall along
dirt roads I was wild to learn these names,

drove alone to that little-traveled patch, filled
notebooks. Even years when I couldn't,
the notebooks, the thought of that place, filled.

You can't return, I know, but when I recently did:
everyone wants a piece of the pie now,
everyone wants country quiet,

the road smelling of ordinary street.
Ditches now behave, now mowed. I've read
in battlefield states, people are paving over

the Civil War, building homes and bike paths,
abutting the nation's history. They're hungry
for souvenirs, for a piece of the action.

Here, in the wide-open spaces, we dig
then preserve the remains of prehistoric animals,
our museums once displaying bones

of the first people. Years ago, a wise man told me
the hillsides of my home county near the Missouri
were dotted with the graves of Native children.

It's not the same, the farm I can't return to,
from the road everything looks different. The town
has shrunk, even their voices strange.

Things change: same house for thirty years,
I now look out at mature *Picea, Quercus, Acer,*
native grasses and forbs I collected before

they disappear. Here, rooms have changed,
habits, too. We no longer dine at the kitchen table
after our son moved away.

I'm no longer the kid sister my brothers once
teased—still younger, somehow wiser—no longer
know them any more, not really, yet

in this new room with its wild view, I'm no longer
the person who would never have believed she
would sit here, pen in hand, wild as sumac to write.

DEAD OF WINTER

In the fire of summer, it's difficult to recall the dead
of winter: green excess, stomata and chlorophyll
on overtime. Humidity swelters along, lifting the skirts
of spruce, their blueness a shimmer, as were

my father's eyes under the brim of his cap,
a tuneless language I perfectly understood. On a
break from the tractor, in the shade of the rusty truck,
we drank a communal jug, consumed the sandwich

wafer, prayed for rain. I still pray for rain, to fill this belly
of occasional drought. When I picture my father in summer,
he's all sweat and rolled sleeve, denim and endless dust.
Winter meant the newspaper, easy chair, pinochle.

Did my father ache for another life, as I sometimes do,
whole days disappearing, like migrant birds, into sky?
Spring rolls around again, the miracle thing. By summer,
under an unrelenting sun, how does anything survive?

In his 50's he whirled from farmer to wage-earner,
whistling. He liked the city, I think, gazing out windows
under new rafters, the roof not in need of immediate repair.
No livestock anywhere. Worked his flowers while he could.

Retirement the last indignity he was forced to swallow.
He hung on until spring, just as iris were breaking dormancy,
bees going at it again. I like to think of my father in winter,
the miracle of all-outdoors at rest, yet utterly alive.

PALIMPSEST

I live in skin handed down from a long line of Danish farmers,
from women and men of the soil, all imperfect, the genetics
of the double recessive all vulnerable and hard at work.

Scrape away the layers and there's no writing anywhere to be found,
only dust and feeder calves and slough grass, the callous of contour,
fertility and row crop. Deep down, beneath this veneer of city

dwelling, there's a well above an aquifer, hand-dug, lined with layers
mortared in place as the water rose up, brick by brick, by Father,
his face with the grin I've inherited, repeating that yarn.

Blotches over his leathered arms and face, his eyes shallow pools
of blue, my father wrote his story all over that farm, not an acre
untouched, loam plowed, trees planted, hogs slaughtered.

Fence posts. Corn, wheat, oats. Outbuildings that rose
board by board into sky, a young girl breathing haybale
and clover blossom and top soil, gritty as our old dog Brownie.

And a grandmother who longed for the homeland, the home place
that won't quite collapse. My child's child, near sleep, wanting me
to retell the youth of her father, the time of her birth, her smooth hand

squeezing. Squeezing beside my father in our living room recliner,
the recliner he later whiled away the days in. By now I've grown into
his frame, wiry, aging toward the epidermis that was visible from

his casket, the parchment I was afraid to touch. And yet:
grandmother, father, me, son, granddaughter — stories I'm writing
in blood, passing down, layer into layer, better than skin-deep.

White Lie

.

WHAT I DID

What I did I did because of the dirt,
the cattle and the moonless nights.
Because of the open breathing cornfield
and the sounds of roosting hens in the brooder house.
Pears hanging in the pear tree, ripening,
bees drunk and tainted with pollen.
Because of snow storms and power failures
and standing on top of ten-foot drifts.
Because of manure and rutted mud roads
and a dozen mewing kittens, eyes wide,
hungry for the teat. I did what I did
because of a hot breeze on a hot night
when the house wouldn't cool down,
because of home-canned peaches
and a '39 International rusting
in the grove. Because I was alone,
walking in the pasture alone,
studying the creek for anything alive.
Because of the corn crib with its ladder
and heavenly mystery, its unshelled ears,
all listening. Dust and diesel fuel and dumb
lazy afternoons. I did it because of pine needles
and columbines and tiger lilies, because
my grandmother came to this treeless land and lived.
I was alone in the brome, in the ditches and high up in the maple.
I stayed there until I was called in, stayed there
where the branches held me, stayed there
and stayed to hear the wind talk back to me.
I did what I did because I thought everybody did,
counting the large coins in my father's drawer,
standing in the dark closet to smell mothballs.
I didn't know. I didn't know what any other child knew.
I knew the claw-foot bathtub and the one glass
at the sink we all used. I knew the creak of each step
on the staircase and where to step so it wouldn't.
I was awake when I should have been napping,
up in my room instead of lying down,
looking around during the Sunday prayer.
I played with the cats, an old deck of cards,

with the unmatched unfinished blocks of wood.
The nights held eyes though no one was around.
The dreams were nightmares even though I was loved.
The hay grew tall and we always had enough to eat.
I did what I did because my father loved me, my mother
was occupied and my brothers didn't want me around.
Because of Brown Swiss and John Deere and Hampshires,
neighbors down the road and a one-room country school.
Because of ice cream and watermelon and green apples,
because of fudge and popcorn and wax paper.
I played alone in the silo, in the cellar and on the screen porch.
There were comic books and Lincoln Logs and rollerskates,
bicycles and sand piles and Tinker toys.
What I did was simple and dirty, requiring time alone.
There was no one to talk to, no one to listen, no one to ask.
I wore hand-me-downs and five-buckle overboots,
dresses and saddle shoes, barrettes and anklets.
We ate potatoes and beef, tomatoes and pork,
chicken and dumplings. We went to church. I studied the Bible.
I studied my numbers, my alphabet, my spelling.
My teachers said I daydreamed, wouldn't pay attention.
Alone in my bedroom, in my parents', in the barn.
They hoped I would never know.
Because I wanted, it happened. I did what I did
when it was time, I put in my time when I had to,
I lived through it.

UNDERGROUND

There were ghosts underground,
that much was certain.

Years ago we'd stop there,
the abandoned farm place

where only trees pulsed,
my father moving about

under their coolness,
their delicate webs.

Was it here his siblings died
in infancy? Was it here

he was born? He never said.
A place stuck out nowhere,

the faucet of rushing memory.
My brother and I were told only

to watch out for the old well, don't fall
in. That nub of fear all it took

to prevent us from running.
Those yellow afternoons:

touch of nettle, whiff of lost
beginnings, taste of mold.

THE OLD BARN

1.

I see my brothers in the hayloft with kitchen matches
and tin, striking and taking turns, yellow flames licking.
Smoke curling up, ashes floating down the hay drop.

The overhead cave where we inhale field dust,
where the rope pulley-hook lilts along its full length,
where the feathertips of a bowl-faced barn owl

sweep past, a ladder rises from composted manure.
We are unable to halt the siding from its own ignition,
the ancient supports, 12 x 12's, a cottonwood tinderbox.

How will we extinguish it without being caught?
What will we explain to father, returning from the field?
We all believe in God and right now He is not happy.

2.

They immigrated to this country for farming and freedom,
grandfather first, returning to fetch his young first cousin.

Grandmother isolated and frightened, this treeless flatland.
No one warned her about raking weather, the relentless wind,
no one knew of drought or typhus or how to save the children.

The new barn, its beckoning rafters, the only height for miles.
He kept the spare rope with him, hidden under the wagon seat.

My brothers and I tasting fear, smelling our own small demise,
one after another calves in the feedlot loping toward pasture.
The air full of shouts, Father from a distance detecting trouble.

If our grandparents survived grief and nature, why can't we?
Water holy from the stock tank hitting the blackened wall.

DUST

The issue at hand is dust—dust off the nearby soybean field
being harvested, field unclean with its Russian thistle, its
buttonweed, its endless unwalked rows. Dust rising, haloing
the early evening sun. A full harvest moon going soon to hunters,
moon the Lakota called Moon of Changing Seasons. Farmers
harvesting by its light, by rigs equipped with headlights, with what
my father never owned. Outside of chores—feeding and milking—
he never farmed on Sunday, spoke ill of neighbors who went
to the field instead of church. Perhaps he needed a break from all
the dust, from hayfever and allergies, the coughing and wheezing
and constant drip. How often did he drag himself outdoors to get on
with the work, what kept him going all those long hard lean years,
years we could barely scrape up an extra dollar. Dust following
the corn picker and the combine, dry field dust, dust of chaff, corn
crib dust, feed-grinding dust, haybale and haystack dust, dust
in the barn loft and brooder house, dusty cattle yards, dusty
implements, dust of the forge, dust and cobwebs in the machine
shed, dirt floor dust, coal dust, dust in the cellar, dust of pesticides,
dust in the air, on the clothes and in the mouth. Plowing fields
in a dry spring, dust blowing through the house. A life that was all
dirt and corn, hay and livestock, a life of dust. Dust off evergreens
—pollen—yellow dust in the air. Ragweed and mold spores and
dust mites. Breathe it day into day. Earth to earth, ashes to
ashes, all of us soon light enough to be carried aloft by the wind.

HOW MY DOLL STOPPED
SPEAKING TO ME

I can still see him.
He strides away from the house
over knotweed and gravel
in sweaty denims without looking
back. He shakes his seed cap, disappears
into the barn's non-judgmental mouth.

From the kitchen sink,
my mother watches him
through the window, muttering
his name into humid air.
The supper plates are stacked, waiting.
An acrid taste of change on the tongue.

With one hand she wipes a soapy rag
over and over the same spot, the other
pushes hair off her damp forehead.
This time the bank has refused,
and she didn't want to hear it, it's no use,
there's nothing, nothing more to say.

VETERANS DAY

By the time I came along the war was legend,
Its submerged evidence washed up for me to learn:

Mike's father with his flash-burned eyes, a first cousin
Dead at Pearl Harbor, the rag-tag veterans parade

At our hometown Decoration Day. I studied the shadow
Of cultural hatred, the philosophy of patriotic zeal.

Each year brought the cut opulence of common
Blooming things — flags, ferns, sickly-sweet peonies —

Each observance a raising of rifles and salutes,
The lingering of sulfur, the lonesomeness of taps.

But more than anything I tasted the sad luck of blood:
My father — too old for this war, too young for the first —

Exempt, suspended in that awkwardness of time,
Serving his country stuck in fields of corn and wheat,

His rank at the helm of a tractor, his hands grasping air
In the empty maneuvers of his unspoken grief.

CLASSICS

In Israel, chickens increase egg production by 6%
while listening to Mozart—NPR news

Long-haired music, my father called it,
dismissing it all with a wave of his weathered hand.

If we'd had a spare radio, most likely it would have been
Glenn Miller or Tommy Dorsey or Lawrence Welk

piped into the henhouse, those dusty Wyandottes
in their straw-lined cubicles, gullets and gizzards

at work on our breakfast. No such research then,
only oyster shells for calcium, debeaking to keep

the pullets from plucking each other. Oh, let me
call you sweetheart: chicks downy in a peeping box.

Lights, feed, feathers. Eggs in the morning, eggs
in the evening, eggs at suppertime. The egg and I.

My heart going where the wild goose goes, Frankie.
Roosters strutting in the yard: home, home on the range.

Squawking and crunching and flopping headless;
Mother wielding a bloodied axe. That old silver-haired

daddy of mine: now is the time we have to say
good-bye.

WHOLE SUMMERS

Whole summers were like this:
a rock garden thick with tiger lilies and weeds,
robins bobbing heads into thin grass,
a lilypond blooming with green algae.

Some windless days in near-stopped time:
a girl and her dog wandering from house
to grove, past a shaded cemetery where pets
turn to compost, past barnloft,

                              through the alfalfa
field and pasture, sidestepping dung piles, following
a cow path past the windmill and stock tank
and gawking heifers, down a cordgrass swale
to circle back —

              shortcut through nettles
and barbed wire, over a ditch to the county road,
the girl killing time, in the heat leading her
pooch toward the farm place

                          like relatives
returning after a long-lost absence, walking
down the gravel lane and up the rock path,
lighting on crude log chairs,

                      surveying
the gardens that were surely a refuge to her
homesick grandparents, viewing them now
in mid-century ruin,

                      the elaborate overgrown
scheme of iris and peavine and redstone enough
almost to one day break her heart.

THE LESSON

One late night when you're eight or nine
    your older brother comes home to the farmhouse
        drunk, only you don't know it at once,

what wakes you in your upstairs bedroom
    is clumsy footsteps on the ascent,
        commotion in the bathroom, shouting.

Under the blankets, you're afraid to breathe.
    You've never heard your father's voice enraged,
        don't yet know blackness holding such secrets.

Why do your parents drag you into that bedroom,
    insist you witness? The hall light yellow on mother's
        nightgown, over the broad of your father's back.

North wind rattles the windowpanes; you shiver
    and shift your toes. What could you learn beyond
        the sprawl of this sibling: leaves scattering

from grove to barnyard to fenceline, your brother
    cowering, crying, your mother crying, your father,
        leather belt now slack at his side.

ENDLESS SUMMER

Back where everything is flat:
the adolescent, her feet sore, rolling
counterclockwise under the bare lightbulbs
of the rink.

    Teen angel, can you hear me?

What is she searching for? Why do
rented skates always pinch and blister—
scuffed white for the ladies, black for men?
The high-school drop-out smooth as glass,
a curving stream backward, jaunty forward.
The girl trying not to fall, pushing her straps
behind the sleeveless dress. Socks too thin,
nails poking into her soles, eyeglasses
slipping down her nose. Around and again
to the Shangri-Las, hoping not to be bumped:
one collision, a whole gang takes a dive.
Smudges across the yellow dress, bruises
on the knee.

    Teen angel, can you see me?

Around and around until the couple-skate;
a few shy pairs, hand in hand, glide onto
the horizontal world under a sparkling orb.
In a dim corner, a basketball player tests
the boundaries of a cheerleader's blouse.
Outside to inside, losers—town guys
going nowhere—pass a bottle. Glow
of Lucky Strikes, smoke in unmoving air.
A four-barrel Biscayne shifts its Hurst,
burns its racing slicks through the park,
rumbles the throat of its glass-packs, its balls
of fuzzy dice.

    Are you somewhere up above?

Soft streetlights, the sounds and smells

of leather and lagoon and laughter.
A dry town surrounded by level dryland.

Are you still my own true love?

                    Look,
see her there on the side, waiting, unable
to articulate desire. And later, outside
the cafe, after curly fries and Cokes, waiting
for her brother to drive them home where
their mother waits up in the dark farmhouse,
the girl her whole life anticipating something
words will not properly take shape around,
will never stand up, shake off the static dust,
roll away from.

VICTORIA'S SECRET

is what we longed to unveil,

how lace and satin and décolleté
in apricot or coral or hunter

could succeed knit and white and undershirt,
our own bodies budding into possibility,

chemise and strapless and side-slit
nowhere in our lexicon,

our mothers shopping for us
in catalogs of Wards and Sears,

cinched as they were in gartered girdles
and their no-frill brassieres,

sheer and plunge and highcut
decades away,

dreaming not in silk pyjamas
but cotton nighties,

cropped and gauzy and thong
as foreign then as *natural*,

candle and sage and blush not yet colors,
our underlying ache desirable

as, before the eyes of the world,
we ripened, pure and green.

HAILSTORM, 1965

Q: *What is the largest hailstone in the U.S.?*
A: *There have been six reports of hailstones eight inches in diameter.*
                                     —The Weather Channel

It was the summer I turned sixteen, one brother
was soon to be married and we'd sold the farm.
I remember wanting desperately to be kissed.

Everything wavered on some kind of edge, elm trees
a graceful dome over the dusty streets. Nothing to warn,
only cumulonimbus clouds in the afternoon, intense up-

drafts, sky hazed sulfur-green, hail starting as crystalline
seeds that grew to marble-size, geometrically then,
to the size of softballs, clattering heavy against metal,

wood, glass, against the only small world we knew.
All the west windows in the high school, every roof,
field corn stripped down to stubs, lives shattered

that day by crop failure, gouges, even holes in the ground.
There had never been any guarantee. Always there is
a risk, a gamble, hard choices to make. My oldest brother

and I scooped out stones that ripped through
the ragtop of his '62 Impala. I can't imagine hail the size
of a melon. Somehow that day I sensed that youth

had dissipated, that through the vapor of downed leaves
and broken branches, there would always be another crisis,
another close call, and yet there was something more out there

circling, the open road where I drove west — my oldest brother dozing
in the passenger's seat, my learners permit in tow — eighty on I-90
toward Missoula, toward the end of what we know now as innocence.

WHITE LIE

It must have been summer, breeze fluttering the curtains,
old beds made up out on the screened-in porch. Long
ago, yet I remember my first one plain as day: No.

Not out of fear, really. My mother's face flushed,
asking Did you come out here? I was supposed
to be napping after lunch, my father always did,

except for this quick chance on the fold-down divan,
Father in his work clothes, Mother in her apron, while outdoors
cottonwood leaves moved in their rubbery dance.

What could've I said? Not guessing until much later
what they were up to, laughing out loud at this one:
Why don't Methodists make love standing up?

Oh, the things we talk about when we can't talk about
certain things: weather, the price of cattle, the twister in '59
that took out the neighbor's barn.

I couldn't sleep, must have heard, peeked, father's hands
busy on her backside. Father, who, wanting the facts
from my brothers, would say, Now don't tell a story,

meaning don't tell a lie. We were all meat and potatoes,
taking great effort to conceal all passion. Yet
I was safe that day under the tent of pretense,

the one where things don't exist if they're not discussed.
No, I said. I smelled rain and went outside, I said. That fall,
our banker having loaned us even more on the promise

of record yields, we'd watch the red afternoon sky for missiles
from Cuba. We believed our teacher when she said
no one will get hurt beneath the desk. Nothing to fear

in God or government policy. Put enough sugar on rhubarb,
you make it edible. Because it too closely resembles
dancing. And that's the gospel truth.

Crossing a Footbridge

IN PRAISE OF THE TEMPORAL

—beginning with a line by Larry Levis

Elegy for whatever had a pattern in it:
a web, a spider, light over the one lying in bed.
Sun through windows of the bedroom, warming.

The way it slants on the walls, rosier than terra cotta,
lighter than Pipestone—blood and bones of ancestors,
place where native tribes came together in peace—

a shade of earth to grace the new remodeling.
And so it arouses me to see him, roller in hand,
paint on his shirt and pants, late afternoon sun

on plywood floors in the new addition, over bare walls.
He grins, globs of drywall compound on the old carpet.
Your clothes are down the basement, he says.

He's removed the ceiling trim, revealing a strip of gray.
So ugly, some of that room's old faces, times we differed.
I see his face, the walls a pipestone-terra-cotta-peach.

Yesterday, he donated blood, his pressure down.
Smooth as brandy, the late afternoon sun. Stubbly
beard, holy jeans, t-shirt. All day working up a sweat,

glancing out, all day wings past windows, two hawks
landing. Running errands for lumber and paint, hauling things.
So many years in the same house, in this room a quarter-

century of sleeping and dressing and undressing.
In two days new carpet will arrive, two days to trim and finish.
Now the tang of new paint, the strand of possibility.

DOVETAILS

At the Shaker exhibit my husband marvels
    at orderly elegance, at the unadorned beauty

of hardwood furniture fashioned by hands, hands
    attempting perfection under the watchful eye of God.

A craftsman himself, he covets the clean lines,
    the impossibly thin pins and tails—dovetails—jointing

the drawers, hand-chiseled, prudent and simple.
    With a fluttering of his hands he tries to illustrate,

but it's his fervor and pitch that persuade me,
    permit me to stand at the foothold of enigma,

to wonder what compels some creatures to live in communes,
    celibate, what surely propels others on wings through air.

And when he leans in for a closer inspection,
    a bizarre and distant voice admonishes

Do Not Touch the Exhibit Please Stay Two Feet Back
    as if it's consummation itself—fanning its feathers,

bobbing its head, calling to a place where passion dwells—
    material witness in its fine and delicate bones.

OUT HERE

Out here on the edge
of town where the half-moon
spreads its half-light,
where the shallow creek
runs deep into the heartland,
where deer at this hour
have already stepped away,

I'm for no reason awake,
the form next to me a metronome,
breathing, thinking
of that hour before slumber,
the hands, the lips,
the familiar
tangle,

and those other times
in other towns where creek
becomes river, its water swift,
where all manner of things disconnect,
wandering their curious streets,
their anonymous woods, where
we indulge in what they claim to offer,

stoke the fire,
sink into its warm springs
these unforgotten limbs,
these silent tongues,
all contours symbiotic,
my worn response somehow new:
Oh! Oh! Oh! Oh! Oh!

BUILDING A HOUSE

everything is on hold
everything in your life
all summer on hold
including your old toilet
making that water sound
& the bowl seeming fuller
than it should be &
when you ask he says
the guts need replacing
the internal mechanism
the toilet-repair-kit-gizmo
& you say you know
& he says there's only one
of me there's no time now
& that's how it is everything
on hold because the new house
the rush the push the race
now to get it enclosed
tonight just finish up the shingles
on the east end of the south side
toward the peak just a few more
feet just about an hour of sun
maybe tonight we'll do it
then there's the ridge cap
piece of cake comes in
ten foot lengths a cinch
then it's done all roofed
all insulated R-11 R-30
all plumbed all electrical
all heating all framing
2 by 6's 2 by 8's 2 by 10's
all fitted all inspected
now drywallers now the front
storm door gotta get it stripped
just one more layer of paint
already got maybe five off
down to fir down to wood
yes we're down to something
solid something old something
shithead Dale took off & discarded
when he started remodeling

now who would throw away
a perfectly good wood storm-
door who tell me who
those suckers'll cost you
major bucks this one'll be better
than that crap they advertise
this one has class this one
once all that gunky paint
gets off will be but to envy
better than new about the age
of the front door off the Chism
house set aside the beveled glass
stripped off 80 years of varnish
down to solid oak with three tall
lost art glass panels true art
best thing to come out of that
whole house that front door
before they bulldozed it
& now it'll go on the new house
have a new life be ten times
better than the cheap stuff
they charge an arm & a leg for
so you see there's no time
for the toilet for a bike ride
for doing it for doing anything
got away once this summer
took one trip one 24-hour ride
to Kansas City the only chance
& wouldn't you know it
there was one of those archi-
tectural salvage warehouses
& it was like he'd died & gone
to heaven doorknobs grillwork
wooden doors windows fireplaces
you name it phone booths fences
chairs tables light fixtures the
whole mess all of it just waiting
to be measured & claimed
for somebody's new house
somebody's remodeling project
toilets sinks banisters newel
posts the whole damn she-bang

sensory overload to a born-again
recycler a pack rat a person
who drools at the sight of
quarter-sawn oak like there's
a serious shortage of it
like the things you could do
with all that stuff redoing it
not to mention the sheer beauty
the way they used to make things
back in the old days the old way
the solid the real none of this
flimsy stuff no ornamentation
no frilly useless decoration
just rock-bottom durability
not like that furniture Larry & Liz
bought looked nice for awhile
made of teak veneer—*shiTEE*—
but the third or fourth time
we moved it fell apart
held together with staples & glue
glue & sawdust so much
of the new furniture nowadays
looks OK at first then it falls
apart so you see we've got to
get back got to return to the real
the authentic & there's no time
getting closer just a month maybe
right after kitchen cabinets
measuring & fitting & building them
the siding the inside & outside
painting & staining right
after laying that oak flooring
board by board sanding it by
god slapping on a gym finish
better than anything new you
won't be able to take your eyes
off it & we'll have it done
we can do it we can do it right
it'll be worth it I know I just know
we can do it oh baby

CRANE-DANCE

At dusk along the Platte wave after wave
    of sandhill cranes wing their way lower—

drifting, arching, stilt-legs extending—
    landing their bones hollow into shallow water.

Their great noise must be in celebration,
    voice joining voice, tallying who made it

this far, this half-way stopover on the narrow
    flyway, enroute to northern mating grounds.

All night in the sandy riverbed clamoring,
    overhead stars illuminating a rural sky.

An urge older than imagination. Watching,
    I can't help thinking biology and love,

how genetics prove efficient on behalf of species.
    A scientist might define it—the crane-dance,

the lively display of feathers for a beloved—
    as programming. Yet the mystery, the rush:

in your eye a look, a signal, in your body
    a call, a scent, all around the loosening,

the melt, the unrestraint of near-spring,
    on the horizon a cradle moon, bone-thin.

·

FULL MOON, LATE SUMMER

full spinning wheel moon
Canadian geese skimming treetops
crickets thrumming for mates
northern cold front diving
you me diving ah blanket
in the night you me your warmth
your hands in the night your legs
I'm dreaming you dreaming skin
your full length next to mine pulsing
into morning ah sweet morning
fog spreading over milo over wet
grass hovering fog a wet blanket
above creek you hovering you
and sun sweet sun cherry ball
rising rising

MY HUSBAND SPEAKS OF WOOD

It's all there he says
In the grain
The story of the tree
Its stresses
Its imperfections
The thick of rain
The thin of drought

Burl and pattern and knot
How some woods age smooth
Filled with grace
How maple sometimes goes
Birdseye
Others split and pockmark
Beyond salvation

Feel this he says
It's walnut smell it
Juglans
This pine
Resin
Or this cherrywood
Call it sweet

Wine aged in oak
Taste it
The tannins
Wood and beer
Their grain their
Pigment their
Texture

I'll rip these two
Plane them to hear
A distinctive resonance
Show you bookmatching
With tung oil finish them
Wait!
I'll show you

ON MEDICINE BOW PEAK, WYOMING

–USGS marker: 12,013 ft.

On a clear day
you can see forever
almost — south to jagged peaks in Colorado,
west and north to more Rockies and basins,
east to the Laramie Range and beyond
with its slow descent onto the Plains —

the ground below frostline
spread out like a geological feast:
igneous, sedimentary, metamorphic —
underlying rocks revealing some of Earth's
least-known stories,

the horizon playing tricks on your perceptions,
its witchery of light and shadow, of glittery
glacier-carved lakes, snowfields and quartzite,
the wind steady in your face, you
in thin air weighing heavy

concepts of time and nature and what
came before and what will after,
so you simply take it in — crunch
and salt and all your brain can grasp,
the grin of your buddy climbing
bringing you almost to tears.

IN A LUNAR YEAR

Summer Solstice
In the Rockies on Medicine Bow Peak,
we hear the splinter of lightning
before the clap, sense the red thread
of our spines while clambering down.
We are fleas to this mountain,
fork-fodder to its god of atmosphere.
Later on this longest day, we laugh,
recalling the close call, munching gorp
from our over-prepared pockets.
Later, breathing the relief of campfire.

Fall Equinox
When a northern cold front whistles
across the Plains, even the insects
pay attention. Crickets stroke their bellies
for mates, spiders spin webs indoors,
lowly boxelder bugs flock beneath
house and barn siding for warmth.
The ash tree now a yellow yard antenna,
signaling the movie: Day Equals Night.
Spice of apples from the orchard.
Ground dew greeting the dawn.

Winter Solstice
From County Galway, I pen postcards
with icy fingers on this shortest day,
rise late for the full Irish breakfast.
The windows last night a touch
of frosted mirror. Yet stone walls
along the narrow roads and fields
create a patchwork quilt, even in winter
emerald green. Domestic sheep the essence
of damp wool in the rain. So what sound,
perhaps, to make me move? Crowbar.

Spring Equinox
The bubble of winter thaws, refreezes,
its pops and clicks and longer sunrays
key-touch to our light-deprived minds.
We can almost savor the salad

rising from loam, whiff the paint of sky
beyond tender leaves. Today the sun
crosses the celestial equator, that yellow
calf with equal dark and light spots.
Mother Nature herself at work:
hiss, gurgle, wind, warmth, flower.

MORNING WALK

You don't ever know where
a sentence will take you... —Mary Oliver

Before sunrise under the halogen hunter's moon,
an autumn morning stretches ahead of me, a rhythm:

shy stars over the city, the inky dark, the concrete path on which
I pound out duty, conjure up fantasy, those old tensions;

in the street, vehicles sounding their singular verb — speed —
on the other side, at season's end, the syntax of wheat field,

muslin consonants remaining, its vowels of harvest long gone.
At times I'd like to stick out my thumb, that potent comma,

to risk all for a sentence into the unknown — who knows where
it might lead — to those other lives scattering in each direction.

But soon enough a string of nouns pulls me back, keeps me
moving on the straight and parallel, leads me home again

where through my wild yard at first light the quick red fox
bounds, its fluffy tail the ultimate dash, the unanswered question,

where gathering blackbirds as if on cue swirl up sudden,
excess ellipses peppering the sky.

WINTER ON THE PLAINS

The earth turns green again,
no matter what. —Walter McDonald

Morning light a dull window:
when I raise the blinds
an overnight snow falls into frame.

No forecast, no disruptive wind,
now just a half-inch of fresh powder
over every last branch and twig.

A month ago in a gale I gripped a handrail
at the Cliffs of Moher, felt the Atlantic pound
angry the face of west Ireland.

Salt spray and sea foam and ancient walls.
The fields emerald, even in winter,
each square foot parceled by stone.

Here, stubble pokes above a white layer,
grass weighs bleached in the ditches.
Here, where rain and ice and snow

are capable of conspiracy, cohorts of
heat and drought and tornado, lovers of
dun prairie. Yet the earth turns green again,

no matter what. I stare at a textured canvas
over which blobs of bright Pollack paint
now move: chickadee, cardinal, jay.

BEFORE DAWN NEAR SALT CREEK

Something wild and footloose here, in shadows
beneath the over-sized, up-lighted beer sign
along the four-lane highway
at the edge of urban sprawl,

not the taste of fear, not
ominous shadow or startling,
but this: four deer standing
in the inky ditch, upwind,

where I have stopped, just over the footbridge,
just another middle-aged walker,
ogle-eyed in the oncoming headlights,
unmoving, not like when the unshaven man

stepped out of this thicket last week,
bedroll like a turtle strapped to his back,
but for a spell watching each other,
ears twitching in the nervous dark,

death and exhaust going 50
not fifty feet away, munching,
until they bolt over fence into trees,
tails high and white,

and I tip my head, move on,
toast our co-mingled breaths, now rising.

SUMAC SCATTERING LIKE BONES

When a sheepdog goes off alone to die,
do you suppose he believes his survivors won't suffer?

Maybe the dog and all pets comprehend their presence.
The message in their eyes and tails—almost human—

commands us; their primary flaws lean to excessiveness
and unquestioning loyalty.

Mostly, he was all hair and wagging. Even when he heaved
blood throughout the basement, we couldn't bring ourselves.

He chose the fern bed, cool and damp, where for years he'd
dug and trampled. Where mosquitoes could do nothing more.

We buried him beneath sumacs. Cinnamon ferns,
true to their ancient spores, unfurled again from loam.

Each fall the backyard, having flamed, drops its leaves.
All winter from inside the house we gaze out over ribs.

TOWARD MOONSET

Walking toward moonset I watch the dancing man,
his movements barely perceptible, yet there
within that perfect globe sinking into a navy horizon.

What puzzles me is that others don't seem to notice,
why drivers don't stop or at least slow down.
Is it just me, helpless again, lost in memory
or its merry sidekick, anticipation?

I think of father teasing me, teasing out,
over protests, my dimples, in his own manner
telling me how much I meant to him. Now,
I'm surrounded: the imprecision of language,
this relentless, metaphorical season.

I declare the snow, sparkling under sodium vapor,
to be spun wool, fields—a powdered sugar
fallowland, dark lumps hunkered down on the creek—
lovers on a waving waterbed. The forward/reverse
of a distant snowplow becomes last night's rhythm—
over the back, between the legs.

Turning, sunrise must be somewhere,
brightening the cloud-hung eastern sky, street-
lights switching off, snowdrifts going white, dry.
Traffic increases—splattering from tires,
the slush, the gravel.

What was it the agronomist said—dirt is merely
soil out of place? Over my shoulder, the dancing
moon grows yellow. Ahead, a small ground blizzard
blots the path. Silly me, taking this desolate wind
for a love song!

BEFORE DAYBREAK

Before daybreak, a few laggard geese
 on mired water, ice coating the sandbars.
  Vehicle fumes, incessant whine of tires.

Lone foot out in front, then the opposite—
 intensifying speed, uncracking joints,
  burning thighs. Sweat beneath abundant layers.

All brittle and drab, all frosted roofs and scraping
 windshields. Reports of digging out in Dakota,
  mudslides and floods way west, a blizzard down south.

Desiring coastline, ocean slapping the shore,
 undulating waves. Falling asleep to the cadence,
  waking to its brine, water and sand between the toes.

A truck driver offers a hoot. And there, aloft—
 matched geese—unflapping, deliberate, overlapping,
  two dark rags in the air. Why don't they fall?

Did they run off together in the dead of winter, can they
 be mating? In nature, beauty equates soundness.
  One foot, then the other, over this concrete treadmill.

Recalling dreams of danger, exaggerated slowness
 while trying to escape, how at the prevailing moment
  you elevated above earth, an inventive getaway.

Now, a day-glo sun plods upward. The earth tilts,
 geese nowhere near. You are destined some-
  place, you tell yourself. You are, you are.

DUCKS WALKING ON WATER

Are all of them, after all, holy?
  Waddling, they seem proud of themselves,
    knowing sandbars in dull water.

Geese, fewer of them now, moving
  out of the weather, overhanging branches
    ribs on a dark umbrella.

Flapping, honking, restless off the riverbed,
  trying to decide: this field or that,
    one direction or reverse.

Only last week the wind numbing,
  prodding myself onward, limbs stiffening:
    how easy, slowing easy, to stop moving.

Sleet pinging off cheeks, on tongue.
  Vehicles, their uneasy perfume.
    Snowdrifts shrink, no hiding, no escape.

Moon this morning a thin slice perched on the lip
  of a lemonade sky. Grayness not fooling,
    earth-hiss, moisture into the air.

Is not the universe expanding, ever increasing?
  Yes, I believe it's coming back to me:
    ducks walking on water,

that one green reason for not giving in.

AT ROWE SANCTUARY ON THE PLATTE

Not the blind leading the blind, but our guide
leading in late afternoon in a pickup off the highway,
down mid-March mud roads, past snowdrifts and farmsteads,
hiking then to an inconspicuous box on stilts of plywood
near the river:

                     we go to a blind in order to see
what a guide promises—mallard, merganser, muskrat—
offering knowledge as we brush shoulders, stare
through portholes at swift water just thawed,
exchange stories with strangers,
watch beaver

                  work the treeless bank,
raccoon lumbering in the shallows below,
my husband leaning toward me, whispering how it smells
like a river, meaning it smells like his childhood,
those late summer nights with gear and lure and pole
and his long-gone father,

                         while the sun bends
down yellow to flame, a hawk loops low over sandbar,
Canada geese take a chance and land in the channel,
and we can now hear them—sandhill cranes—at dusk
rising in great waves from stubbled fields where
they glean energy, our guide says, from waste corn,

calling in high raspy voices, circling, gliding in groups,
landing down and upstream, louder, then closer,
their sound going from the ear into the conscious,
you forget the gathering cool, the rapid loss of body heat,
under the ancient formations Leo, Canus Major, Orion,
cranes by the hundreds, by the thousands

                       land,
stilt-legged in the shallow Platte, their noise in near-dark
so wild, so redeeming you cannot hear normal speech,
even if you could close your gaping mouth, think
of something near-intelligent to say.

PHILOSOPHY, EARLY SPRING

This isn't exactly the butterfly effect — all morning
red wings bumping against the bedroom window,

one cardinal in his persistent folly — no
enormous impact to the world because of it,

but maybe it's the prior knowledge that soon
he'll grow weary, unselect himself right out

of the gene pool. Is it my fault, having formed
a greenish habitat here, complete with mirror?

He emerges from a branch of the honeysuckle,
time and again, hovering and thumping into glass,

nothing to block this reflected apparent rival.
Perhaps I should inject my own outlook,

cushion such stubbornness. My gray cat
ever the hunter, crouches, smelling stew.

Tender leaves flavor this protected corner,
new bird sounds shout into blue air. But

spitting song doesn't guarantee happiness; why
would I wish to alter the odds? Soon I'll dig,

plant and water, bullheaded in the belief that
hope — in all its jellyfeathers — springs eternal.

DEER AT DUSK

Low in the darkening south sky, the young moon curves
into a bone-thin saucer, Venus beside it
a sharp and unblinking eye.

Here, where feedlots stink the otherwise unsullied air,
on the transcontinental passage known as I-80, I negotiate
truck traffic and watch for deer, trying to imagine

what life must be like on dying farms off in the distance,
yard lights cycling on, this stretch through flatlands
engineered to avoid anything eye-catching.

I remember, as a child, traveling on two-lanes
or gravel, peering in. I think of stories, too, my father
in Wyoming smashing a deer, totaling our '49 Ford.

Every mile or so, I'm reminded by dried blood-splatter, by fresh
and wildly scattered parts. Here, in the wide-open spaces,
deer must negotiate great distances in the dry and cold.

Here, with the tree-lined river off to one side,
I follow the tracks of animals that became footpaths,
then wagon trails, gravel, now four-lanes with vehicles

hell-bent east or west, on pavement that heaves and cracks
in weather extremes, concrete that's been patched, repaired,
resurfaced, even replaced in its short-lived existence.

They say there's too many deer. It's nearly 500 miles
across this state. Where was it I read: two hundred years ago
the fastest mode of transportation was the horse?

When I spy them in a field, grazing like cattle,
I'm already past, headlights probing the primitive,
the unforgiving dark.

CAMPING, LATE SUMMER

Late August
waving its wet handkerchief
into the over-heated atmosphere,
this state park sandpit
teeming with a final week
of freedom.

Another summer gone,
leaving its wild-scented carpet:
goldenrod, ragweed, catkin residue
floating lightly on the green-
brown water,

the brief intensity of *here*,
of *now*, that all
on this temperate plain
is but temporary.

So when clouds build
and lightning strikes near the river
we aren't surprised—
cottonwoods thrashing, wind
a cool-diving wall in every direction—

yet wary, wondering
what it must have felt like
earlier this summer
lying next to the man killed
in a tent when the tree fell,

was it in this same area?
the woman with him spared,
asking like we all do, why—
why him and the dog,
why not me?

THE MORNING AFTER

The morning after
I am suspended somewhere
between the moon and the sun, pacing
on autopilot the cold early-autumn air,
cursing the roar of rush-hour,
yet grateful for this hiker-biker trail,

the footbridge over Salt Creek,
and there in the dark water
the great blue heron, sleek and elegant,
back from her summer travels,
bringing a chill, as did last night's total eclipse,
while cars went about their usual business,
oblivious,

like a recent morning in fog
when a woman driving east snaps a quick photo:
behind me the sun rising a perfect blood-red,
so I walk backward a while,
hoping the world will slow down,
this moment fading in only moments,
the story these days of our disconnected lives,

as this morning after,
the sun not quite up and over the west horizon
that wafer-thin-huge-flat disk sinking
into the earth's tongue of atmosphere,
and I want to shout to all the speeders,
to all the hurry-up-or-I'll-be-laters,

before it's too late: the moon! the moon!

FIRST FROST

...*come close to Nature. Then...try to say*
what you see and feel and love and lose.
                —Rainer Maria Rilke

It's as if the sudden change has sharpened things,
this microcosm at first light below a footbridge
on the edge of city-sprawl in the middle
of the mainland:

beaver at the point of a vee in brown water,
its naked scaly tail trolling the shallow creek,
now diving above wavy mud, paddling then
along the grassy bank,

and upstream through pillars of fog I recognize
the silhouette of heron, unmoving in the warm water,
and from a scrub elm, its roots clinging to steepness,
a kingfisher dives, hovers, plunges, emerges,

my eyes on all this until the cold seeps from handrail
metal through my mittened hand, and I see again
along the high embankment a figure hauling
its bedroll, turning east away from me,

man who, as the innocent child points out, is lucky
to be alive, and I agree, love, I agree, child
with her arms around me in this heated shelter,
her adorable yet changing face raised to mine.

MONDAY, SNOW

Through glass in the living room,
where the view is flat sky tangled with limbs,
songbirds crowd the feeder.

I perch on the sofa's back watching
with two granddaughters, wide-eyed,
attentive, like cats, all eyes and ears.

Though they are young, the girls know
these birds mostly by name, most of them black:
red-winged, starling, grackle.

The birds bunch and jump in the cold weather
as if uncertain of their next meal,
cackling for survival, while

the girls chortle and point,
all arms and legs. They're growing at a pace
swifter than I can comprehend.

I recall my mother telling of
her youth, so many mouths to feed it meant
some nights going to bed hungry.

The blackbirds flap-rise in an abrupt swirl
as if to thrill this small audience: shrieking,
falling back over the cushions.

Cardinals dart in for a meal, sparrows, too —
Harris and white-crowned — snow a steady
reminder of an indifferent world.

O my sweet ones, these are matters of life and
death, aren't they. I wish for you what all my mothers
wished: for air, for wings.

SAVING ROOM

When my young granddaughter at the dinner table
announces she's saving room *right here,*

pointing to her side, for dessert, we break out
the cookies. Room enough for a small treat,

room enough for love — that non-fattening, non-
dairy topping, the low-cal, low-cholesterol additive,

nourishing, place next to the heart where all things
are possible — morning, noon and midnight

in the garden of good and evil, that many-splendored
thing, between the devil and the deep blue sea.

When I was young my father asked which half of me
belonged to him, which half belonged to my mother.

My seriousness caused him to grin; I never chose.
He's been gone a decade now. Now, after eight decades

my mother is learning how to dance. Foxtrot and waltz
and two-step, my arthritic, stoop-shouldered mother

gliding in some stranger's arms across a wooden floor.
The heart, that unexplored universe, ever expanding.

Her face, in telling us, beams radiant. I wonder: will I,
too, some day? Take a chance on love, the song says.

Love is a four-letter word, says another. And only fools
rush in. Yet — just in case — I'm saving room *right here.*

GREAT BLUE HERON AGAIN

This morning I see the great blue heron again,
its stilt legs straight out behind as it flaps overhead,
over footpath and creek,

              effortless through early air,
over power lines, around obstacles, and I contemplate
how death might come to a wild thing.

              Yesterday,
I watched my mother struggle to stand on braced legs
in a walker, face drawn forcefully up,

              her upper limbs
flimsy in therapy, her independence so suddenly shifted
down.

When I go to water her houseplants, a small rabbit
in the front flowerbed darts away on three good legs, its
rear appendage an albatross,

              and I think how this creature
won't be long for the world. A hawk, perhaps, another unlucky paw
joining the piles of small fur beneath the backyard ash.

              Today, though,
I shake off the savagery of beak and claw, the randomness of bad
luck: it's heron again as I walk

              and shiver and suck in dry earth
at the sight of great wings rising, silent, what's left of my tongue
recalling a residue of grace.

CROSSING A FOOTBRIDGE ON SALT CREEK
EARLY MORNING IN MID-AUGUST

This time the great blue heron doesn't take flight.
Below: shallow water, sandbars, bottom mud.

It poises motionless, not two hundred feet away,
most of its tarsus submerged. In heron-eye, I'm fluid.

I recall the ducks floating away, another sort of flight
from danger, frogs at a pond's edge, wary, blending in.

What bird would choose to fight? Crows, perhaps: dive-
bombed once by adults when I walked near a fledgling.

Last night the Green Corn Moon rose mottled-orange
between treeline and clouds—heavy summer-squash—

Jupiter constant to the east-southeast. Here day and night:
toads, small fish, crawfish, aquatic life befitting a spear.

Last week I watched a belted kingfisher perch
on its small syndactyl feet above this stream, plunge

then headfirst, rising with a meal in its heron-like bill.
It's taken my whole life to become this harmless.

Coda

WE ARE ON NINE-MILE PRAIRIE WHEN

the news reaches us of twin towers and collapse,
walking with fourth-graders through tall grass,
our guide uttering bluestem and goldenrod, mammal
and snake, this early report not yet registering,

the sun high, burning. Standing on the unplowed,
the whole, no broken sod or surreal debris, only silence,
learning pollination and forb, coyote and mouse,
deer and split-hoof adaptation. This unspoiled place

a split screen — reels replaying later — spider and insect,
growth points above or below, roots with tentacles deeper
than imagination. How do we comprehend fanatics? Out here
we speak French — *prairie*: treeless meadow, evolving

through the millennia. Plant, animal, weather intertwined,
on each other dependent. The first people and fire, following
the source. Fourth grade, when school grows more complex,
when the curriculum includes heritage. How do we define

fear, the future, the dead? The blameless children, rabbits,
bolt from predators, crouch in grass. Nowhere to run, nowhere
to hide, no superman to reverse the earth's rotation, start
this day over. Wings in the air, the claws of terror. We pause

on thatch in the brief quiet, breathe unsullied air. While
winds blow our way, we search for words, phrases,
language that is truly alive. Are we safe on this, our only,
planet? Each child becoming the smallest prey.

9-11-01

CPSIA information can be obtained at www.ICGtesting.com
Printed in the USA
BVOW04s2153301113

337775BV00001B/107/P